ISBN: 978-1-3999-6736-5
Text and illustrations by Siski Kalla

First Edition, 2023

A SHOE is to CHEW

A dog's first book of definitions

A shoe is to chew.

A chewed shoe is to...

... say sorry with a paw.

A paw is also 'please'.

A head tilt is to be irresistible.

And a leash means adventure!

A window is to WHEEEE!

A tree is to say 'I was here.'

Dogs are to sniff.

Dogs are also to play.
And to howl...
sometimes to growl!

A butterfly is to prance...

And to dance...
always just out of reach.

A squirrel is to bark, to bork and BORK and BARK some more!

A hedgehog is NOT to touch.

A frog is to look.

A ball is to follow
A ball is to race
A ball is to borrow
A ball is to chase!

A stick is to never, EVER, let go.

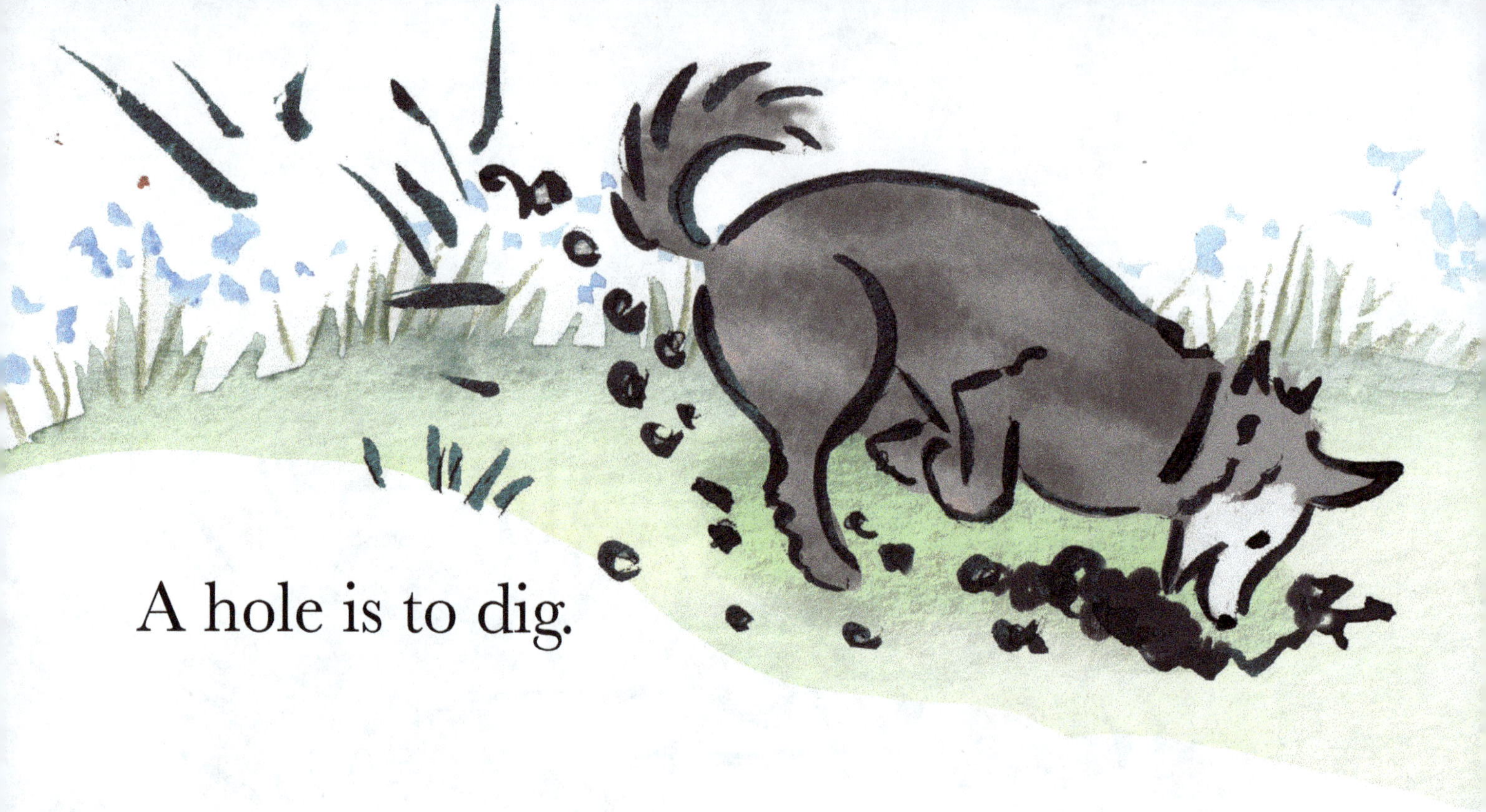

A hole is to dig.

A hole is to stick
your nose in.

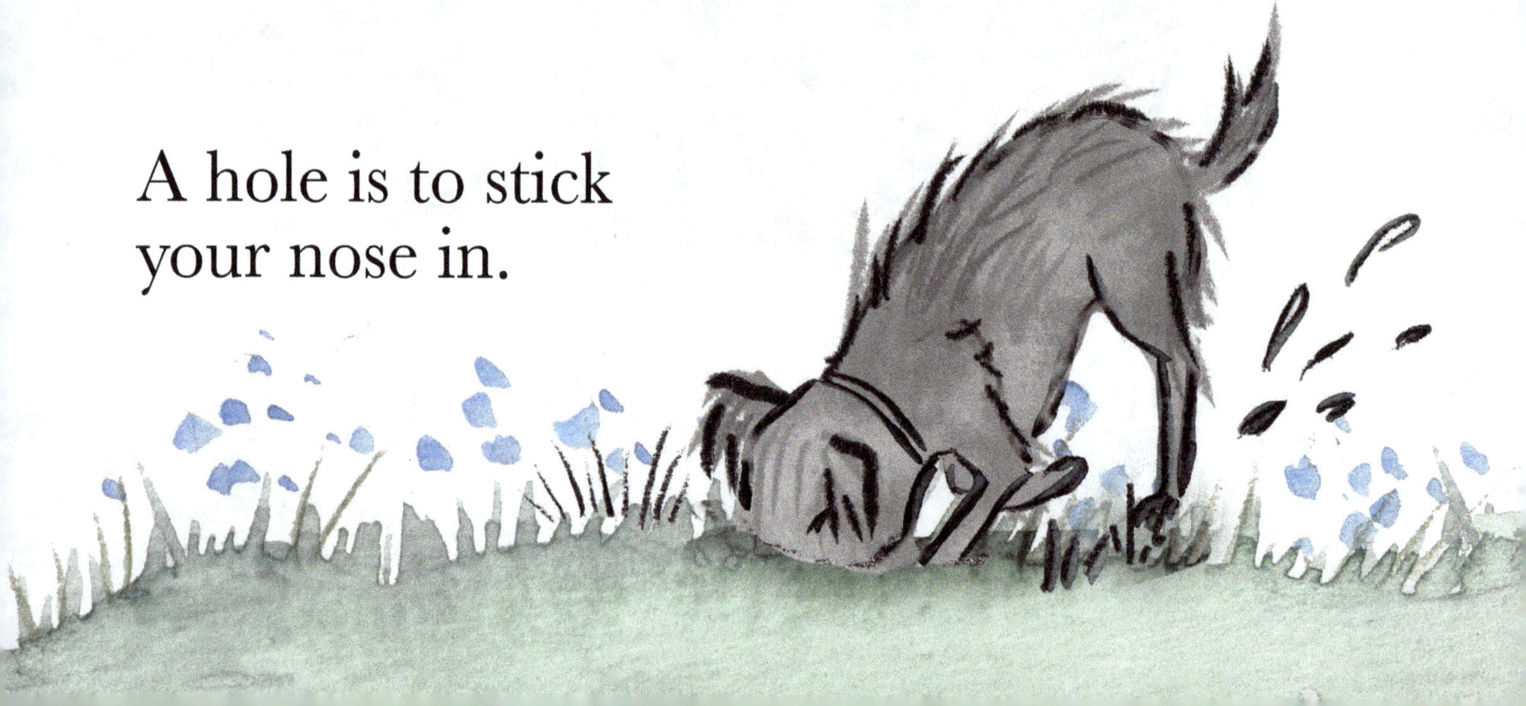

A hole is to save for later.

A hole is to stay cool.
Or warm.

A hole is everything!

Mud is to be happy.

Stinky mud is to be **overjoyed**.

A clean floor is for showing off your mud.

A tummy is to tickle.

And tickle some more, please.

A table is for food to fall.
A baby is for LOTS of food to fall.

Sticky fingers are to lick.

Mlem,
mlem,
mlemmm.

Toes are for saying, 'Wakey wakey!'

A sofa is to snuffle.
A human is to snuggle.

You are to LOVE!

Name(s):

How we met:

Your favourite thing about me:

My favourite thing about you:

Cheeky things I sometimes do:

My favourite place to be:

My favourite word:

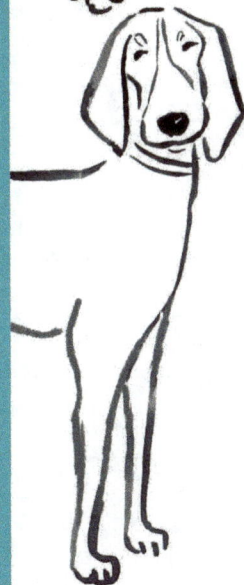

Your dog's photo here

www.ingramcontent.com/pod-product-compliance
Lightning Source LLC
Chambersburg PA
CBHW050633150426
42811CB00052B/778

9 781399 967365